Flute / Oboe Grade 1 - 2

Meet The Great Masters!

18 Favorite Classics for Young Players

*Arranged by
James Curnow*

CURNOW® MUSIC

Order Number: CMP 0520.00

Arranged by James Curnow
Meet The Great Masters
Flute / Oboe

ISBN 90-431-1019-1

CD number: 19.013-3 CMP
CD produced by James L. Hosay

James Curnow

James Curnow was born in Port Huron, Michigan and raised in Royal Oak, Michigan. His formal training was received at Wayne State University (Detroit, Michigan) and at Michigan State University (East Lansing, Michigan), where he was a euphonium student of Leonard Falcone, and a conducting student of Dr. Harry Begian. James Curnow has taught in all areas of instrumental music, both on the public school, and college and university level.

James Curnow has become one of the world's most prolific writers for concert, brass bands and orchestra. He has been commissioned to compose over one-hundred works for band and various ensembles. Curnow's published works now number well over four hundred. Averaging eight to ten commissions a year, of which at least four are major works, Curnow's music is performed all over the world.

Available Books:

Flute/Oboe - CMP 0520.00

B♭ Clarinet - CMP 0521.00

E♭ Alto Saxophone/E♭ Baritone Saxophone CMP 0522.00

B♭ Tenor Saxophone - CMP 0523.00

B♭ Trumpet - CMP 0525.00

F/E♭ Horn - CMP 0526.00

Bassoon/Trombone/Euphonium BC/TC - CMP 0524.00

Piano Accompaniment - CMP 0527.00

Meet The Great Masters!

 Ludwig van Beethoven (1770 - 1827) - Ode To Joy
Born in Bonn, Germany and died in Vienna, Ludwig van Beethoven was born into a family of musicians who had served at the Bonn court of the Elector of Cologne since 1733. He was a master of the symphony, string quartet, and piano sonata, who bridged the Classic and Romantic periods in music. By the time of the premiere of his Symphony #9, which he conducted, he was completely deaf.

 Robert Schumann (1810 - 1856) - The Happy Farmer
Robert Schumann, born in Zwickau, Germany and died in Bonn, studied law at the University of Leipzig, but spent most of his time studying piano and composition. His music was important because it expressed the deepest spirit of the Romantic period.

 George Frederic Handel (1685 - 1759) - The Harmonious Blacksmith
George Frederic Handel was born in Halle and died in London, England. He was known as an outstanding organist and composer. He is considered to be the innovator of England's oratorio and a giant of the late Baroque period.

 Johannes Brahms (1833 - 1897) - Hungarian Dance #5
Johannes Brahms was born in Hamburg and died in Vienna. He was considered to be one of the greatest German composers. He was a master symphonist of the late Romantic period and composed significant works for voice, piano, orchestra and various small ensembles.

 Modest Mussorgsky (1839 - 1881) - The Great Gate Of Kiev
Modest Mussorsky was born in Karevo and died in St. Petersburg, Russia. He was part of the Russian Five (Balakirev, Borodin, Cui, Mussorgsky and Rimsky-Korsakov). The Great Gate of Kiev is a movement from his piano suite, Pictures at an Exhibition.

 Arthur S. Sullivan (1842 - 1900) - Onward Christian Soldiers
Born in London, England, Sir Arthur Sullivan, together with his collaborator Sir William Gilbert, became internationally known for their comic operas. Their first successful work was H.M.S. Pinafore (1878) which led to a very financially rewarding career in theater productions.

Antonin Dvorak (1841 - 1904) - Largo *From the New World Symphony*
Antonin Dvorak was a Czechoslovakian composer who played violin and organ, and through his music established a strong Czech Nationalistic style. From 1892 to 1895 he spent time in The United States as composition teacher and director of the National Conservatory of Music in New York. During this time he composed his Symphony #9, "From the New World", from which this theme has been extracted.

Track 10 **Jeremiah Clark (1674 - 1707) - Trumpet Voluntary**
Jeremiah Clarke was an English composer, and organist in various positions including Winchester College, the Chapel Royal, London and St. Paul's Cathedral, London. His best known and loved work is this Trumpet Voluntary, which was originally published under the title, "Prince of Denmark's March."

Track 11 **Franz Joseph Haydn (1732 - 1809) - Theme From the Emperor Quartet** - *Austria*
Franz Joseph Haydn was an illustrious Austrian composer, the first master of Viennese Classicism and the "Father of the Symphony", of which he wrote over one hundred. This melody became the Austrian national anthem.

 Wolfgang Amadeus Mozart (1756 - 1791)- Theme From Don Juan
A prodigious Austrian composer, Wolfgang Amadeus Mozart's works, of every type, are unsurpassed in lyric beauty, rhythmic variety and effortless melodic invention. This delightful melody is taken from his comic opera, Don Juan (1787).

 Henry Purcell (1659 - 1695) - Trumpet Tune
Henry Purcell, a composer and organist, is considered to be one of the greatest of all English composers and an outstanding figure of the Baroque period. This Trumpet Tune is one of his most popular works.

 Felix Mendelssohn (1809 - 1847) - Hark! the Herald Angels Sing
A German composer, pianist and conductor of enormous talent, Felix Mendelsshon achieved great success during his brief lifetime. The exact origins of this melody are unknown.

 Track 15

Giuseppe Verdi (1813 - 1901) - Triumphal March

Giuseppe Verdi was a great Italian composer whose genius for dramatic, lyric, and tragic stage music has made him a favorite of opera enthusiasts. This melody is in the style of a processional march.

 Track 16

Johann Sebastian Bach (1685 - 1750) - Minuet

A German composer, organist and pedagogue of high esteem, and a giant of the Baroque period, few of his works were published during his lifetime. This simple yet elegant minuet is just one of many that he composed during his career.

 Track 17

Edvard Grieg (1843 - 1907) - Sailor's Song

Born in Bergen, Norway, where he lived and composed most of his life, Edvard Grieg is known mainly for his songs and short piano pieces, and his love for Norwegian folk music. This melody is from a collection of piano pieces.

 **Track 18**

Tylman Susato (1500 - 1564) - Rondo

Little is known regarding the life of Tylman Susato, other than the fact that he was a Belgium composer, trumpeter and publisher of musical works. His Rondo melody has been popular through the centuries, as a theme for variation by numerous composers.

 Track 19

Georges Bizet (1838 - 1875) - Toreador Song

A French composer, pianist, conductor and organist of world renown, Georges Bizet's opera Carmen did not become readily accepted as a great work until after his death in 1875. The Toreador Song has become one of the best-loved songs from the opera.

Track 20

Richard Wagner (1813 - 1883) - Pilgrim's Chorus

Richard Wagner was a great German composer and conductor who's monumental music dramas, written to his own librettos, radically transformed the concept of stage music. Hoping to conquer the musical society of Paris, France, Wagner premiered Tannhauser in 1861 to mixed reviews. Later it went on to become one of his most beloved operas.

Contents

MEET THE GREAT MASTERS

Arranged by
James Curnow (ASCAP)

FLUTE
OBOE

Track **3**

Ode To Joy

Ludwig van Beethoven (1770 - 1827)

Track **4**

The Happy Farmer

Robert Schumann (1810 - 1856)

The Harmonious Blacksmith

George Frederic Handel (1685 - 1759)

Hungarian Dance #5

Johannes Brahms (1833 - 1897)

The Great Gate Of Kiev
From Pictures At An Exhibition

Modest Mussorgsky (1839 - 1881)

Moderately fast (♩ = 112)

Onward Christian Soldiers

Arthur S. Sullivan (1842 - 1900)

March tempo (♩ = 108)

Track 9

Largo
From The New World Symphony

Antonin Dvorak (1841 - 1904)

Track 10

Trumpet Voluntary

Jeremiah Clark (1674 - 1707)

Theme From the Emperor Quartet
Austria

Franz Joseph Haydn (1732 - 1809)

Theme From Don Juan

Wolfgang Amadeus Mozart (1756 - 1791)

Trumpet Tune

Henry Purcell (1659 - 1695)

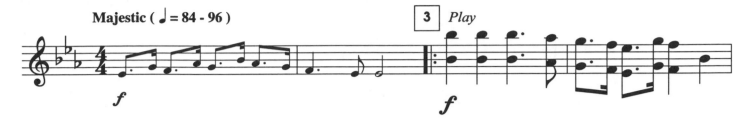

Hark! the Herald Angels Sing

Felix Mendelssohn (1809 - 1847)

Triumphal March

From Aida

Giuseppe Verdi (1813 - 1901)

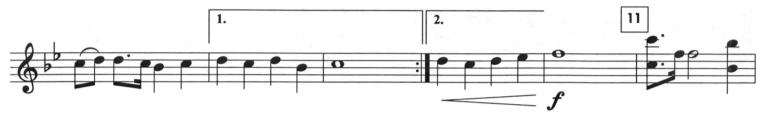

Minuet

Johann Sebastian Bach (1685 - 1750)

Sailor's Song

Edvard Grieg (1843 - 1907)

Rondo

Tylman Susato (1500 - 1564)

Toreador Song

From Carmen

Georges Bizet (1838 - 1875)

Moderately fast (♩ = 104)

5 *Play*

f marcato

1.

2.

Pilgrim's Chorus

From Tannhauser

Richard Wagner (1813 - 1883)

Majestically (♩ = 80) **3** *Play*

f   *f marcato*   *3*

11

p

18 *Rall.*

cresc. *3*   *f*